Mother to All,
Mother Forever

Series Preface

The volumes in NCP's "7 x 4" series offer a meditation a day for four weeks, a bite of food for thought, a reflection that lets a reader ponder the spiritual significance of each and every day. Small enough to slip into a purse or coat pocket, these books fit easily into everyday routines.

Kathleen Ahoul

Mother to All, Mother Forever

Four Weeks with Mary of Nazareth

Megan McKenna

New City Press
Hyde Park, New York

Published in the United States by New City Press
202 Cardinal Rd., Hyde Park, NY 12538
www.newcitypress.com
©2009 Megan McKenna

Cover design by Durva Correia

Library of Congress Cataloging-in-Publication Data:

McKenna, Megan.
  Mother to all and Mother forever : four weeks with Mary of Nazareth /
Megan McKenna.
      p. cm. — ("7 x 4")
  ISBN 978-1-56548-316-3 (pbk. : alk. paper) 1. Mary, Blessed Virgin,
Saint—Meditations. 2. Catholic Church—Prayers and devotions. I. Title.
  BX2160.23.M45 2009
  232.91—dc22   2008053419

Printed in the United States of America

Contents

one
Mary, as Daughter, Mother, Wife

two
The Mother Who Walks with Us in All Seasons

three
The Lady of Thresholds and Gates

four
Everyone's Lady, For Always

Foreword

Pope John Paul II writes of Mary, who, in John's gospel (Jn 19:26), stands witness at the foot of the cross:

> She is Mother to all and Mother forever. The goal of her mission is to reproduce in believers the features of her firstborn Son (cf. Paul VI, Apostolic Exhortation *Marialis cultus*, 57), bringing them at the same time to recover ever more clearly that image and likeness of God in which they were created (cf. Gn 1:26).

The faithful know they can count on the heavenly Mother's concern: Mary will never abandon them. By taking her into their own home as a supreme gift from the heart of the crucified Christ, they are assured a uniquely effective presence in the task of showing the world in every circumstance the fruitfulness of love and the authentic meaning of life.

The woman who contemplated her newborn child with utmost awe and sheer delight is also the woman whose soul was shattered as she saw the horror of hate that destroyed the body of her beloved child grown to be a man. A simple definition of contemplation is a long, loving look at reality, especially reality that is hard to look at. The soul of Mary contemplates God becoming flesh in the world and, like her child, grows "in wisdom, age, and grace" through that mystery of contemplation.

May the meditations offered here accompany you over the next four weeks, and may the woman who so loved the Word lead you to "Do whatever he tells you" (Jn 2:5). And may you live on the Word of the Lord so that it takes on the flesh of your own life.

Mary as Daughter, Mother, and Wife

one

1 Anne, Myriam, Joshua

Mary is Nazareth's faithful daughter, the ark of the covenant, the root of Jesse, and Joshua (Jesus), the word of the covenant, is born of this woman. This is faith's ancient history, genealogy, going backward and forward in grace and time. This is the "house made of dawn." Like the dolls that Russian and Greek craftspeople have for centuries nested one inside the other, one generation is nested inside the other, layer upon layer of promise given to a people, of hope in each generation, and hope brought forth in the person of Jesus Christ, yesterday, today, and forever.

Anne is known only in tradition, like so many other anonymous mothers. But Jesus, born of a woman betrothed to Joseph, is Jewish through his mother's line and blood ties, through her human flesh, though divine in promise and his Father's long invisible love.

This "trinity" blends the towering strength and wisdom of the Old Testament with the incarnated tender and mothering wisdom of the New Testament. The child is the seed, the fruit, and the core of the women's flesh and of all history.

Daughters of God, who taught the words to one another across the years, teach your great-great-great-grandchildren now. Teach us how to pray, how to pass on the best of our tradition and faith to one another. We trace our roots back to your own, in covenant, in creation, and in the human community.

Prayer: Seat of Wisdom, grandmother, daughter-mother, serpentine graces, seeping through the ages with longing, passing on life, teach us to see in every face both young and old, the marvels of God being revealed in our times. May we your children by redeeming grace be offspring that surprise you with gladness as once your firstborn brought you unbounded joy. Let us sing with you: O bless the Lord, my soul, and all that is within me, bless your Holy Name. Amen.

2 Mother of Our Lord

Elizabeth is in wonderment as the presence of God comes to visit her and Mary's greeting sounds in her ears, stirring even her child to recognition and joy. "Who am I that the mother of my Lord should come to me?" (Lk 1:43). Mary's voice uttering the ancient greeting "Shalom" (the peace of the Lord be with you) is like an electric current jolting John — the one who goes before the Lord — awake, alerting him to immediacy, to the nearness of the Word made flesh, sleeping and growing in Mary's flesh.

The Word of the Lord, in Gabriel's Good News, has come to this young woman and she is "good soil" — like those who "upon hearing the Word, hold it fast in their hearts and bring forth fruit with patient endurance" (Lk 8:15). She is an Israelite, one who waits on the Word of the Lord, staking her life on God's faithful promises. Like Abraham, she endures with her people, but now she knows God's time has come. And now every greeting, every word that comes forth from her mouth, is like dew on the ground, rain in a parched land, hope for dried up and shriveled hearts that have so long sought the coming of the promise into their lives.

This child she bears is the ancient Word: "Yahweh our justice" (Jer 23:6), who will right the flawed universe and hearten the poor with justice. She is hopeful that we will hear the Word of Good News to the poor, release to the captives, recovery of sight to the blind, liberation for the oppressed, and a year of mercy from our God, who is Lord of all by right of justice's love.

Prayer: Mater Domini, mother of Our Lord, plant and nourish the seed of God's great reversal of fortunes in your children's hearts. Make us strong and steadfast, a people of enduring faithfulness who hear the Word of the Lord and let it take root in us. May we be people of peace who know, with you, that Our Lord is Yahweh Shalom, and this child is the Lord of our hearts. Amen.

3 Mother of the Incarnate Word

Rabbi Abbahu said in the name of Rabbi Yahanan: "When the Holy One, blessed be he, gave the Torah, not a bird cried, not a fowl flew, not an ox bellowed, the angels did not fly, the seraphim did not say, Holy, Holy, Holy, the sea did not stir, the human creatures did not speak, but the world was still and silent, and the voice went forth: 'I am the Lord thy God' " (Ex 20:2).

Silently, Mary studies the Word, taking it within herself, holding it dear. The seed is planted; it matures and ripens within her. She will labor to give birth to the Word Incarnate, to freedom and liberation, to a great harvest of hope, to a field of peace, a hundredfold — bread for the world.

Our creeds tell us that the incarnation is a joint work of both the Spirit and this woman. Jesus is born of her flesh and God's breath. And again she is overshadowed by that power of the Spirit at Pentecost where she dwells in the heart of the community of the church as it grows with wisdom, age, and grace, as a fledgling (Acts 1:13–14; 2:1–4). Catherine of Siena writes:

Prayer: O Mary, my tenderest love! In you is written the Word from whom we have the teaching of life. You are the tablet that sets this teaching before us. I see that this Word, once written in you, was never without the cross of holy desire. Even as He was conceived in you, desire to die for the salvation of humankind was grafted and bound into Him. This is why He had been made flesh. Mary, write that Word, carve it deep in our hearts, and make us come true to God's will. Amen.

4 The Holy Family

Mary, Joseph, and Jesus are a family, a trinity, man, woman, and child, but for those with eyes to see there is more: another Trinity lies hidden here, that of the Father, the Son, and the Spirit, the Holy Family, the community of God that is God. This small family lives in the embrace of the Trinity. That is what makes any family holy, any set of relationships holy.

They have presented the child to the Lord, according to their law and tradition, and it is this child who will present their lives to God as worship and sacrifice. Already we are told by the prophet Simeon in the Scriptures: "And this child is the light for revelation to the Gentiles and the glory for your people Israel" (Lk 2:32). Luke goes on to say, "The child's father and mother were amazed at what was said about him and Simeon blessed them" (Lk 2:33) — these parents and this family, called to be light in the sight of all peoples. And Mary is singled out and warned, told realistically, that she will suffer because of her child, this "sign of contradiction": "you yourself a sword will pierce — so that the thoughts of many hearts may be revealed" (Lk 2:35). The life of this family will find its meaning and its pain and its glory in the truth of who this child is, Son of God, Jesus, Word made flesh. This is the reality, the destiny of all families that desire to be holy, to see their meaning in this Word of God, and to share it with one another, letting it reveal their thoughts and lay bare their hearts before one another and before God.

Prayer: Joseph and Mary and Jesus, your family was remarkable for your faithfulness, your trust in God, and your care for one another. Teach us, each of us, in whatever situations our families live, to follow in your way, to be together as light for others and as tightly bound to one another, in the Word of God made flesh, as you were on earth. May we hope to share in the glory of your family, the glory of all the kingdom of God, and the glory of those who have gone before us in faith and those who will come after us. Bind us together forever in your trinitarian love. Amen.

5 Mother of God

Mary knows the ancient prophecies. She contemplates their realities. She, who even now rejoices in life, remembers the original birth pangs, the terrible death pangs, the victorious tearing pangs of life opening the womb again, eyes again, prisons again.

Life and death provide such a jumble and tangle of limbs and loves and human beings, God's wonders, our evils, and death's claw — all weaving the rich purple of her mantle of rejoicing. There is no escaping history's claims, choices made, the twisting of the story's beginnings. But then again, there is no escaping the love, the freedom, the rejoicing of her heart in her son's resurrection.

Daniel Berrigan has written a poem based on Isaiah 42:1–7. It is called "In the Beginning":

(In the beginning)
all things left my hand.
You, clay gently kneaded.
Mouth to your mouth, a lover,
I breathed,
you breathed, newborn.

Now hand in hand
we walk the world.
You, as though clean parchment —
my covenant, your flesh writ.
You, living text.
My work, my wonders, yours;
to open blind eyes
to lead forth the captives!
These, yes
ever greater works, await!

Prayer: Mother of God now you invite us to walk the world with you. Give us your unshed tears, your faithfulness to God, your silent witness to God's original hope for all the earth. May our tangled and intertwined lives serve to set the world right and turn all its mourning into dancing. May we all come home together and gladden your heart and wipe all your tears away. Let us together with you magnify the Lord again. May all our spirits rejoice in God our Savior. Amen.

Our Lady of Sorrows

Together with Mary, woman of sorrows, we are called to meditate on the passion of Christ, the absence and the lingering presence of the Crucified One.

This is the woman who knows intimately the old man Simeon's prophecy that was a knife in her soul, a sword in her heart. She knows that association with this child, who was a sign of contradiction, division, and contention, is dangerous. He was the cause of the rise and fall of many, and the sword cut home in her so that the secret thoughts of many would be revealed (Lk 2:34–35).

Mary is the woman wounded by division, by the wrenching choices of those from Jesus' own hometown who rejected him and those who sought from the beginning to kill him by massacring even children. She is the weeping woman who nightly (it is told in stories) cried hot, silent tears with all the mothers whose hearts were torn from them as their children were torn to pieces by the soldiers.

This is the woman whose countenance has been carved by convulsive grief. All the life leaves through her eyes as she watches the blood seep from his rent and torn flesh. This is the woman of Lent, of Good Friday and all the days of death since, when she must stand at the foot of the cross, her arms awkwardly empty, helplessly gesturing toward all those who are her children — the murdered and the murderers.

This is the woman of sorrow, like her son, afflicted with our inequities (see Isa 53). This woman is beautiful beyond telling.

Prayer: O Mother, you wordlessly remind us of all the horror we have done, of our sins' consequences. And yet, you hold us all in your inner gaze, in the deep tear in your heart, forgiving us, as you forgave those who nailed Jesus to the wood of the cross and those who just as surely nailed your own heart to it. *Mater Dolorosa,* never stop looking at us, until we stand beside you and share your sorrow, and know the sword you carried in our own hearts. Amen.

7 Mother of God, Mystical Rose

The image of the Mystical Rose is both ancient and universally known. Rumi, a Muslim mystic-poet, wrote:

A man once asked me, "Is there a way into the Other Place here on earth?" I said, "Yes, there is a door between this room and the other. For every person its size is subtly different, for it has the shape each being makes when on their knees. No one enters the Rose Garden unless lost in adoration and wonder; no one walks through that door except on their knees."

You are — we all are — the beloved of the Beloved, and in every moment, in every event of your life, the Beloved is whispering to you everything you need to hear and know. Who can ever explain this miracle? It simply is. Listen, and you will discover it every passing moment. Listen, and your whole life will become a conversation in thought and act between you and him.

Mary too was created for this conversation. Long before Gabriel bent before her asking the favor of a reply to God's great desire to become one with us in her flesh and the body of her son, Jesus the Christ, Mary listened, tuned her ear and soul to every whisper of the Holy.

Mary's silence grasped the Word of God and allowed the Spirit to transfigure her body and soul, allowed God to borrow her blood and bones and skin so that the conversation between God and all of us, his often deaf children, could be opened and begun anew.

And we are allowed to overhear one of her mystical conversations in Luke's rendering of her Magnificat, when she carried the unopened flower of God's love within her:

> My soul proclaims the greatness of the Lord and my spirit rejoices in God my Savior because he looked upon the lowliness of his servant. Yes, from now onwards all generations will call me blessed, for the Almighty has done great things for me. Holy is his Name, and his faithful love extends age after age to those who fear him.

> *(Lk 1:46–50)*

Prayer: O Mary, Mother of God, Mystical Rose, in your conversation with God you are always opening, just beginning to blossom and giving birth to the Word of God, to anyone who will hear and take this Word of truth and love to heart. Help us to remember that we were made for this conversation with God, with the friends of God, and, of course, with you. Amen.

The Mother Who Walks
with Us in All Seasons

Mother of Fairest Love

I am the Mother of Fairest Love, of reverence, of knowledge, and new hope; therefore I am given to all my children.

(Sir 24:18)

This woman of fairest love is Wisdom described in the Scriptures. Listen: "She is a breath of the power of God, a pure emanation of the glory of the Almighty; she is a reflection of eternal light, a spotless mirror of God's action and an image of goodness. She enters holy souls, making them prophets and friends of God, for God loves only those who live with Wisdom" (Wis 7:25, 26, 27b).

This mother is a gift of God to all of us, calling us to imitate and experience in our relationships of love some taste of reverence, of knowledge, and of holy hope. In honoring the mother we honor the Son; in knowing the mother, we know the Son.

Prayer: O Mother of Fairest Love teach us how to delight in those God has given us to love and those who love us. Help us to reverence them as gifts from God and to know the deep abiding indwelling of joy that is faithful and enduring and in rare moments exhilarating and beyond description. May we live as God intended and share the "fullness of God that we have all received, love following upon love" (Jn 1:16).

Let us remember that we are all children of your beloved son and are given to share of the delicious wine of the one family of God with you as our mother. Dwell in our families, bringing your light and breath, and make us all the friends of God. Amen.

Madonna of the Way

Mary is the woman who first walked the way in Jesus' company, as later others, like the first disciples called in Galilee, would "go off in his company" (Mk 1:18), following him, following the Father's way. Always, those who hear the Word, who are attuned to the Scriptures and learn to incorporate the Word into their own flesh, go off together and live in the company of others searching out wisdom, sharing common life, and supporting one another on this way. It is the way of truth and mercy, the way of justice, the way of "denying your very self, picking up your cross and coming after me" (Mk 8:34). It is the way of picking up the burden laid on those who suffer without cause the grievances of those who do evil.

It is her way, too, from the beginning when she answered Gabriel: "May your way have its way in me, in my person, in my life. May your will come into the world through me. I am your way into the weary waiting world that has been so half-hearted in following you, the world where prophets stumble and the poor drag along, where saints and sinners grow together. Come, this way is open wide to your Word."

Where are we bound, carrying this Word entrusted to us, as company on our way? Is this Word hope for all those we meet along the way? Do our company and our greetings invite the world into the presence of God? Does our way cross through the byways and highways where we bring Good News? Are we bound for glory?

Prayer: Madonna of the Way, help us to embrace the way of your son, the way of God's Word, the will of God even unto the way of the cross. Thus may we walk until we are met on the way of freedom and resurrection by Jesus the Christ walking toward us, wanting our company forever. Amen.

3 Light in All Darkness

Mary is the bright mother, and her child is the light of the world. Both child and mother are flames against the dark of night, the dread nightmares of our times, the nights of despair and persecution of those condemned by others. They are a community sharing bonds of pain and brightness.

They hold us, called in baptism to be candles of comfort and consolation to one another in our pain shared. We have been summoned to bring that light unbroken to the world and to our own deaths — until our lights burn out, impassioned, and come to be one fire in God's great heart.

They are our companions on the way who remind us of the dream. In our times of physical pain, isolation, and trembling fear they will be our healers. In our times of separation from God and one another, they are our communion — a warmth of presence, as darkness gathers around us. But nothing can extinguish this inner burning. The mother and child are given to us as shelter, as a silent blessing on all those who must depend on God, and especially on those who find their sickness and grief, and their time on earth, too much to bear. We are surrounded with and en-circled with love, the love of mother and child, the most vulnerable of loves and the most sure of loves.

Prayer: Mother of God, Light in All Darkness, free us from the shadows of sin and death. Hold our very lives, our bodies and souls, close to your heart until we see the light of salvation and God's glory shining upon us forever. Until then may we imitate your protective attention and bend with care over those whose wicks are short and frayed and whose spirits are bent and bruised. We ask this as children of the light. Amen.

4 Black Madonna

Bright mother, dark virgin, you stand with hands raised in prayer, offering praise, making sacrifice. You stand before the altar; you are the altar, a table spread with the feast of your son. You are the new temple; your body holds the body of Christ, the church, the child, the priest-victim, and the offering of thanksgiving, Eucharist. It is God who has vested you with joy. You gently expose your heart and reveal where you dwell.

In verdant pastures where God would give
us repose, …
you spread the table before us.…
Our cup overflows.…
Only goodness and kindness
will follow us all the days of our life;
and we shall dwell in the house of the Lord
for years to come. (Psalm 23)

You are the compassionate Black Madonna, beautiful and comely (see the Song of Songs). You carry compassion to us and open your arms wide revealing *rechamin* (literally "movements of the womb"), God's mercy (Ex 34). Like Moses, you have seen God and your face is radiant, unveiled. The ancient prayer rings true! The Byzantine liturgy of St. Basil proclaims:

O you who are full of grace, all creation
rejoices in you!
The hierarchies of the angels and the race of
humans rejoice.
O sanctified temple and rational paradise,
virginal glory, of whom God took flesh!
He who is God before all ages, became a
child.
Your womb he made His Throne,
and your lap He made greater than the
heavens.
Indeed all creation exults in you.
Glory be to you!

Prayer: Black Madonna, you invite us to the table, to intimacy and feasting with God and one another. May we sit together around your son and drink the cup of blessing until we drink it with great joy in the kingdom of God.

5 Hail Star of the Sea
(Ave Maris Stella)

This ancient greeting, calling to this guiding star, this beacon that beckons toward home! Mariners, seafarers of old, called a compass "star of the sea" because of its shape. "Is Our Lady the true compass of the Christian life?" (Dame Felicitas of Stanbrook Abbey). The dark of night falls back as Mary and her child emerge in this common brightness, boldly advancing toward us.

All elements of creation — light, dark, water, sky, moon, stars, space, and human flesh — are in harmony. She stands firmly navigating a course through turbulent waters with ease. Hands wide-open, blessing, and moving forward toward us — like the prow of a seaworthy vessel. Eyes wide-open, parting our hearts, intent on entering into our troubled souls and storm-filled lives, during this dangerous gale-battered journey. She hears the murmurs of broken hearts, those who mourn the death of loved ones and who know the tides of despair and the panic of exiles and refugees. And her spirit settles softly over us with calm.

Her child, the Word of God, holds the world, continents and seas of green and blue. This is the child of the mother! Compass steady, four directions holding true, all radiating from one point — the heart-womb of a woman's word — the way to steer home by. This is the mother of the child!

Prayer: Ave Maris Stella, the waters of
   baptism have closed over us,
and we have come up gasping for the fresh
   air of God's Spirit.
Grasp us by the hand, dear lady,
whose waters broke to loose a Savior into
   the world.
Ave Maris Stella,
Ave mother of our maker,
Ave compass of our souls,
make us bold in our belief, playful in our
   hope,
and boundless as the sea of God's love you
   have so openhandedly brought to earth.
Mater amabili, ora pro nobis,
pray for your children who call upon thee.
Ave sanctissima, star of the sea. Amen.

The Holy Protection of the Mother of God

There is an icon which has been revered since ancient times by Greek and Russian Orthodox churches. During a time of terrible danger, a Greek saint and "holy fool," Andrew, and his follower, Eiphanion, were praying in an all-night vigil in a church in Constantinople for deliverance from an invading Slavic army. Suddenly the Mother of God and a great host of heavenly beings appeared in the church above the two. The Blessed Mother held out her veil as a sign to all Christians of her love and protection.

She stands alone, arms raised in prayer, supplication — of God and of us — to stop the killing, the great harm we do to one another, all the while claiming to be her children, forgetting that she is the mother of all peoples. She stands with the cloth draped across her arms as we drape the cross during the Easter season to remind us of the terrible price of resurrection. She is the sign of the cross' power to stop death.

We have not learned. We still go after one another like dogs chewing on flesh and bones. In her sorrow she is always there, where there are battlefields and killing grounds. And her veil is first offered to the victims — beyond nationality or ethnic grouping, beyond race or religion. Her protection, her veil of tears, is for the ones we call enemy, those we treat inhumanly, the ones we massacre in our cruelty, as once her own son was stripped of dignity at the cross and killed. She stands centered, the eye of the storm, begging us to stop, wanting to enfold us with her veil and hold us all together — victims and killers becoming her children again in response to her son's victory over death. She prays to bring us back to life, to imitate her in opening our arms to clasp one another in forgiveness. She is an ambassador for God, pleading for us to be reconciled to one another in God. The Holy Protection Troparion, October 1, proclaims:

Prayer: Today, believing people, let us
radiantly feast,
Overshadowed by your coming,
O Mother of God,
And beholding your most pure image,
Let us say with tender feeling:
Cover us with your Holy Protection,
And save us from every evil,
You who pray to your son,
Christ our God, to save our souls. Amen.

7 Mother of God of Magadan

Magadan is a city in eastern Siberia, built by Stalin as the administrative center of the slave labor camps of the former Soviet Union. It is a place of death where millions were martyred: holy ones of the Catholic and Orthodox traditions, especially three hundred Russian Orthodox bishops who refused to submit. The *perestroika* of unity, of communion of the Eastern and Western traditions of Catholicism, began here. The Soviet Union was once called "Holy Russia"; if it is to be so again, it will be in part because of the blood of so many anonymous souls harvested here.

In John's rendition of the crucifixion Mary is given again a child grown — not only young John but the new family of God, drawn from the side of this man, the body of Christ. She is given the whole church.

And now she is invited to take into her arms all the bodies of those who died unjustly, brutishly in slave labor camps, oppressed and made to bear the heavy burden of oppression (see Ex 1).

Her body holding his is altar and table where "from East to West a perfect offering may be made to the glory of his name," where all may share in the body made the bread of life, "life ever more abundantly for all." The suffering is "finished," yet it is not ended. The kingdom of communion among all those who confess to the Word of everlasting life is yet to resound throughout the world in exaltation.

There is still such vast pain, so many millions slaughtered one by one by one. Martin Luther King Jr. stated:

> Returning violence for violence only multiplies violence, adding deeper darkness to a night already devoid of stars. Darkness cannot drive out darkness; only light can do that. Hate cannot drive out hate; only love can do that. Only love.

Prayer: O Mother of God, dear Mother of Magadan, Mother of Holy Russia, mother of all those disappeared, enslaved, forced into hard labor, mother of those who like your son refused to bend before any god but the God of Life, the God most holy and transcendent, hold us as you have held your flesh in God's body and help us to hold fast to a singlehearted devotion to life, even unto death, and unto life without end. Amen.

The Lady of
Thresholds and Gates

Our Lady of the New Advent, the Gate of Heaven

Mary is the gate of heaven. She is the threshold, the doorway between heaven and earth, between the presence of God invisible and God visible who comes to us as one of us, "like us in all things, save sin" (Eucharistic Prayer 3).

John Paul II called the last decade of the twentieth century the "New Advent" and prayed that this third millennium of Christianity be a new era of faith. But it must be more than that. It must be a thousand years of peace and nonviolence, for in just this past one hundred years we have experienced the bloodiest and cruelest time in the world's history. Since 1900 the world killed and slaughtered more people than had been killed since the beginning of time. This faith must be as solid as the mountains and as enduring and commanding in its presence among others. But it must also be like this woman's faith: resolute, unwavering, contemplative, born of acceptance of and reflection on the long telling of the Word of God in her people's history. It must be a faith seeded in promise and hope, the faith of the prophets and the poor, the faith of the lowly people summoned from the beginning to the feast of freedom, of liberation and joy, and with her son's coming in the incarnation, to the table of the Eucharist.

Prayer: Lady of the New Advent, come! Come into our history with your "Yes" to God's will and with your child who was "obedient even unto death, death on a cross" (Phil 2:8). Come into our church and show us how to be open to the Spirit as the angel announced to you the words, "The Holy Spirit will come upon you and the power of the Most High will cover you with its shadow. And so the child will be holy and will be called Son of God" (Lk 1:35). Amen.

2 The Intercession of the Mother of God of Akita

Akita is a city about an hour's flight north of Tokyo. The word "Akita" has two Japanese characters. Japanese characters are pictograms. The first character (in two parts) represents the fall harvest, and the second represents a field. Outside Tokyo is a retreat house with a wooden statue of Mary, carved in 1963 by Saburo Wakasa. In the early 1980s the statue wept 101 times and also bled from the hand. This phenomenon of weeping statues, or icons, has a revered history in the Orthodox tradition. It signifies the desire of Mary to console those who suffer and are victims of the sin of others and to console her own son, who continues to be crucified in the injustices, evil, and sin of the world.

She has known through thousands of years the harvest of pain, the fields of those who die, the seed planted in the ground to bring forth life, the fire of yearning, and the desire for all of us to be one with each other and with God. She is the harvest, the field, and the fire of God.

And she intercedes with us. She is begging us, pleading for us, entreating us, to stop: to look at what we do and what we have become in contrast to what we were called to be — the beloved children of God, the children of the Crucified One who laid down his life that we might live.

With her outstretched hands she seeks to embrace us, touch us as a mother, as a friend, as a woman of God's will and holy desires. She invites us to stand with her, to stand beside her, to stand together, and to pray with her for the aching earth.

But, even more, she implores us to entreat one another to look at our violence, to see and stand beside those who suffer, to bear in our own bodies the marks of our baptism, the brand marks of those bound to her son, those bound to uncrucify and to lift up and give solace to those destroyed by sin. She would have us stand and pray with her:

Prayer: I am your servant, God, I come.
We come to do your will and to bring life.
Amen.

3 Our Lady of Loreto

We think of Mary's home, the house of Loreto. It must have been a simple dwelling, no more than four walls with a door, a window, and a roof. But the house of Loreto stands for every human being's soul, where our bodies dwell and where God holds us in his hand.

From ancient times there has always been the heartfelt hope that each man and woman would be able to dwell in peace, that all would be able to sit beneath their own fig trees and drink wine from their own vines, and that there would be no war, no destruction, in all the land. And Jesus' kingdom is described as a blessed place where all the birds of the air, the unnumbered scores of sparrows, ravens, and crows, can find shelter in the branches and arms of the mustard tree, grown and spreading out into a canopy and dwelling place secure for all in need of a home. A home on earth, a home in God, a home forever — this is the prayer and dream of all human beings.

Psalm 84 sings:

How lovely are your rooms, O Lord of
Hosts!
My soul yearns, pines for the courts of the
Lord.
My heart and my flesh cry out for the living
God.
Even the sparrow finds a home and the
swallow a nest
Where she may lay her young at your altars,
O Lord, my King and my God!
Blessed are those who live in your house;
Blessed the pilgrims whom you strengthen to
make their ascent to you....
One day in your courts is better than a
thousand elsewhere....
I would rather be left at the threshold
In the house of my God than to dwell in any
other.

Prayer: House of David, cedar of Lebanon, ark of the covenant, sheltering tree, tenement, shack, favela, shanty town, cave, house in a village where nothing good was expected to dwell, encircling arms, we give you thanks for giving God a home in your body. That welcome earth became a home for God and all of us again. May we welcome all on earth into our homes and make sure no one is homeless until we are all safe in the heart of our God. Amen.

The Mother Comforted by Her Child

As a mother comforts her son — so will I myself comfort you.

(Isa 66:13)

God's only begotten, he who is in the Father's breast.

(Jn 1:18)

And Thou, Jesus, sweet Lord, art Thou not also a mother? Truly, Thou art a mother, the mother of all mothers who tasted death in thy desire to give life to thy children.

(Anselm of Canterbury)

God is love. God can only be perceived in love.
Father in his inexpressible being,
Mother in his compassionate pity for us.
In his love for us, the Father became woman.
The great sign for us is this: He who was born.

(Clement of Alexandria)

Mary is the tender mother, the lowly one, the poor woman, the unwed mother, the one watching her child leave her to go into the world, the mother witness to execution, the one watching a beloved suffer and die, helpless, beyond even a sigh, wracked with agony. She is the woman who has lost her child and cannot understand why he would go off and do this to her, causing her such grief (see Lk 2:41–52).

Mary is the woman mourning on the day of death, yet pulled into unbelievable rejoicing at his resurrection.

And this is the strong child teaching the mother. This is the lady of grace, held in grace most free, most humble, most gentle and strong. This is the woman who has known God's will in her flesh — its agonies and its raptures. This is the woman we hail and beseech when we are all in dire need and distress.

Prayer: Our Lady of Grace, Mary, the Lord is with thee. Blessed are you and blessed is the fruit of your womb, Jesus. Holy Mary, Mother of God, pray for us sinners now and at the hour of our death. Lady of grace, hold us, as your beloved son holds you, comforting, turning all your fears and trembling to joy as he heals your broken heart. As children of God, teach us to hold one another, healing and freeing one another from fear and pain. May we know your son, your God, your Father, your Spirit, and you, O Mother, holding us all in grace, until forever. Amen.

5 The Virgin of Tenderness

Behold thy mother!

(Jn 19:27)

Look now upon the face that is most like the face of Christ, for only through its brightness can you prepare your vision to see him.

(Dante, Paradiso, 32.85–87)

This is the mystery of one woman's flesh joined to the power of the Most High, the Father, and overshadowed by the Holy Spirit (Lk 1). This is how our God looks in human face and form. Here is "the image of the unseen God, the first-born of all creation, for in him were created all things in heaven and on earth: everything visible and everything invisible.... All things were created through him and for him" (Col 1:15–16).

And Mary is the woman, beloved daughter of the Father, who was the child's mother, first disciple, dearest friend, and intimate of the Spirit.

This woman is known by God and knows in ways that cannot be expressed, except through silence, sight, and touch. Her child, when grown, taught his disciples in a prayer:

> I bless you, Father, Lord of heaven and earth; for hiding these things from the learned and the clever and revealing them to little children. Yes, Father, for that is what it pleased you to do. Everything has been entrusted to me by my Father; and no one knows the Son except the Father, just as no one knows the Father except the Son and those to whom the Son chooses to reveal him. (Mt 11:25–27)

This is the mystery of knowing the Holy and being known back utterly.

Prayer: O virgin so tender, you carry so lightly the bright holiness of the love of God. You let us see the awesome humility of God made human in your flesh and God's wondrous beauty as one of us. Help us to know your Child-God and to know in our lives this tender regard. May we remember, looking at you and Jesus, that our God has made us to love one another. Let us absorb that love in every part of our being and turn and love one another with that love and turn and love you back. Amen.

Mother of God,
Similar to Fire

O Mother-Maiden! O Maid and Mother
  free!
O bush unburnt, burning in Moses' sight!
That down didst ravish from the Deity,
Through humbleness, the Spirit that did
  alight,
Upon thy heart, whence, through that glory's
  might,
Conceived was thy father's sapience!

(Geoffrey Chaucer,
modernized by William Wordsworth)

Mary is a star that held God close on earth.
A sanctuary for the unquenchable fire of love
— God made flesh in the Son of Man, the son
of Mary. This is the woman who pondered all
these things in her heart (Lk 2:19, 51b). This is
the woman praying; the Spirit praying within
her, teaching her to pray; her child, the life of
God in her, bursting through her flesh. She is the
burning bush that is not consumed, the burning
bush of the New Testament.

She prays in the ancient ways of prophets: to honor God, to raise the poor, to do justice and bring mercy upon the earth. This burns all that is not of God to dust and ash. She is a holy flame burning fiercely to illumine the darkness of evil and sin. Her presence sheds light as her son's side was pierced and blood poured out, unleashing the Spirit into the world.

We are told by the Jewish rabbis: "Now Mt. Sinai was altogether in smoke, because the Lord descended upon it in fire!" (see Ex 19:18). They are telling us that the Torah is fire, was given in the midst of fire, and is compared to fire. As the way of fire is, when one is near it, one is burned, but when one is far from it, one is chilled — so the only way is to warm oneself in the light. In Luke we are told how to recognize the unmistakable presence of the risen Lord among us — "Were not our hearts burning inside of us as he talked to us on the road and explained the Scriptures to us?" (Lk 24:32). This is the woman of the Word, similar to fire, Mother of God.

Prayer: Lady, may you spark within us a desire to pray. Make our hearts burn within us. Purge us of fear and sin. Bless us with the fire of the Spirit that overshadowed you, and ask for us the gift of prayer. May the Word made flesh in you warm us and make us torches revealing God to the world! Amen.

7 Mary Most Holy, Mother of All Nations

Hail! Mary Most Holy, Mother of All Nations. You are Wisdom wrapped in silence and saffron standing barefoot on earth's molten core. You cradle the world haloed in the Spirit's fiery tongues. You are marked on forehead and shoulders, and your eyes summon us to reflect and repent on the fate of all your children. You are standing at the foot of the cross still.

And yet God has clothed you in the soft fiery glory spun of the obedience that was your first garment of grace. You bear us all with the same love you gave your firstborn child.

Prayer: Mother, you still hold the deepest hopes of God for us: "Peace on earth for all upon whom God's favor rests" (Lk 2:14).

Mary Most Holy, Mother of All Nations,
 help us recall that the universe is one song
   of praise,

and we are all created to be the beloved of
   God.
Make us all one in the Trinity.
All nations. No nations. No boundaries, only
   expanses.
No borders, only homelands.
No separations, only communion.
As it was in the beginning. Amen.

Everyone's Lady,
For Always

Our Lady of the Apocalypse

Now a great sign appeared in heaven: a woman, robed with the sun, standing on the moon, and on her head a crown of twelve stars. She was pregnant, and in labor, crying aloud in the pangs of childbirth. Then a second sign appeared in the sky: there was a huge red dragon with seven heads and ten horns.... Its tail swept a third of the stars from the sky and hurled them to the ground, and the dragon stopped in front of the woman as she was at the point of giving birth, so that it could eat the child as soon as it was born. The woman was delivered of a boy, the son who was to rule all the nations with an iron scepter, and the child was taken straight up to God and to his throne, while the woman escaped into the desert, where God had prepared a place for her to be looked after.

(Rev 12:1–6)

Mary is the woman pregnant with the long-awaited Holy One, the hope of the ages. This is the woman "whose womb is more spacious than the heavens" (*Panagia* prayer, Russian).

This is God's "Forth-bringer." She is in mortal danger, about to give birth to her child whose name means "save his people from their sins" (Mt 1:21). She is in labor, horror looming before her — Evil that seeks to eat her child. She must give birth. The time is filled.

God's will and power will be made manifest, made human, for the earth. And so the powers of hate, of sin and injustice, amass together to hinder her from bringing light and grace, the person of God, into the world.

But she prevailed with the help of God and his angels, in the face of brutal massacres of the innocent and political and economic powers intent on snuffing out the life of her newborn and, later, equally rabid in their attempt to malign and murder the man grown to Wisdom, God-with-us, Emmanuel.

With the birth of her child, history shifted and a rift opened in the universe. God's humility and love were let loose.

Prayer: Our Lady of the Apocalypse, "we hail you, O Mother, heavenly being, Virgin-throne of God, the glory and bulwark of the church; pray for us constantly to Jesus your son, our Lord, that through you, we may find mercy in the day of judgment, and attain to the good things laid up for those who love God" (John Chrysostom). Amen.

2 Everybody's Lady

Mary faced the fire often in her own life, even when she was young. She lived in occupied territory with the threat of violence present everywhere, knowing her own life and that of her child were in jeopardy, even before he was born, for under the law she would face death by stoning for conceiving a child while only betrothed. Even the birth of this child is marred by the cries of horror — mothers and fathers weeping at the massacre of their children because of Herod's fear and jealousy at the birth of one who would be the hope of the people, "a leader who would shepherd the people Israel" (Mt 2:6). The prophecy continues with the words "He shall be peace" (Mic 5:5). She is the lady who brings peace into a world beset by terror, war, destruction, and hate. Miraculously she brings life to every situation, every place, every heart. She is everyone's lady. Nothing, no one, is left unheard, alone, or unanswered. Her heart, like her womb, is wider and more spacious than the heavens. It has been opened by love.

Thérèse of the Child Jesus, of the Holy Face, the Little Flower, and Doctor of the Church (1874–1897), wrote the following to Mary:

Prayer: Virgin, full of grace, I know that at Nazareth you lived modestly, without requesting anything more. Neither ecstasies, nor miracles, nor other extraordinary deeds enhanced your life, O Queen of the Elect.

The number of the lowly, "the little ones," is very great on earth. They can raise their eyes to you without any fear. You are the incomparable mother who walks with them along the common way to guide them to heaven....

You, O Lady, by God's miraculous design are mother of us all. O Lady of Miraculous Love, answer our deepest needs and the prayers we cannot put into words. Bring light. Bring hope. Bring peace to our lives and to all the world — again, as once you brought forth your child. Bless us, O Lady, and look upon us with the light of Christ that shines in you for all to see. Amen.

3 Woman Who Lives in Hope

God was first revealed to Moses upon a mountain in the presence of a bush that burned but was not consumed. This bush, this tree of life, was rooted in God's compassion. The announcement "I have heard the cry of my people, enslaved in Egypt, and I have come down to save them" (Ex 3:7–8) was the reason for Yahweh drawing close to earth to speak with Moses. And Moses is sent to liberate the people of God and draw them out of bondage, draw them into the covenant and freedom — making them a people. It was the advent of hope and mercy.

Generations later, God bent down again, intent on coming closer to us, and beseeched a young girl for help in saving the people from their sins. And she stood, attentive and hearing the Word, ready — "Here I am, Lord. May your Word be done in me" (Lk 1:38). Evangelization began with her obedience. She seeks to bring her son — borne in her womb, carried still within her to us — to feed our lives with new fire, mercy's fire. She comes as mother, as sister, as disciple and preacher, as missionary, as the presence of God among us, as faithful daughter of the Holy Spirit, and as a member of the community of believers.

We, like Moses, must come near, come together, redeemed by her son, converted to God's will, brothers and sisters and mothers to her son Jesus the Christ. Words she once heard or overheard him say — "Who is my mother, brother, and sister? ... Anyone who hears the Word of my Father and puts it into practice is mother, brother, and sister to me!" (Mt 12:48–50) — are now put before us. She obeyed and put into practice, put into her flesh and life, the Word she heard. And she set out into the mountains bringing this Word to the house of Elizabeth near Jerusalem.

Prayer: O radiant sign and example of Christian life, awaken a song in us your children, a response to the gospel call to repentance and a burning desire to be reconciled with one another. Yearning for holiness, we unite in prayer so we may be transformed by grace into mercy for one another. Amen.

4 Mother of God of Medjugorje, the Burning Bush (1)

> I beg you, dear children, beginning today, start to love
> with a burning love, the love with which I love you!
>
> *(Mary to visionaries, May 29, 1986)*

Mary, Mother of God of Medjugorje, is a living flame of love. She is a prophet, crying out in the wilderness for humankind to return to God and know the vibrant love that God has always lavished on his people. She is reminiscent of God's presence when the Israelites came out of Egypt, when "Yahweh preceded them, by day in a pillar of cloud to show them the way, and by night a pillar of fire to give them light, so that they could march by day and night" (Ex 13:21).

This passage ends with the statement that the cloud and the pillar of fire never left them. Later in Exodus the people are summoned to the holy Mount Sinai, but are warned not to touch even the edge of it. They assemble and the mountain is engulfed in smoke "because Yahweh had descended on it in the form of fire" (Ex 19:18). The whole event is wrapped in fear and power, barely contained, that shakes the very foundations of the earth. And it is in this atmosphere that God reveals the covenant's binding laws to the people.

This is the revelation for God's people in these days. The cloud hovers over the new burning bush that stands as a fierce candle flame, a beacon bright that is not consumed, but is lasting, faithful. Mary stands again on the earth, bringing Old Covenant and New Testament together in her person. She is a Hebrew prophet and a disciple of the crucified Christ, wrapped in the white garment of those baptized in the blood of the Lamb. In her often-repeated words and presence she summons God's people to once again refuse to serve the idols of dominance, oppression, materialism, and self-centeredness, and to believe wholeheartedly in the summons of God made visible in her child who loved — loved even unto bitter death, leaving us fresh manna, the food of his body and blood.

Prayer: O Mother of God of Medjugorje, shed light in all the darkened corners of our world and help us to heed again the summons of the Word of God.

5 Mother of God of Medjugorje, the Burning Bush (2)

Mary is the Mother of God of Medjugorje whose words are most clearly understood in the tradition of the prophets, psalms, and foremost in the words of her own son, revealing God the Father and the Spirit, the God of the Trinity and community. If we hear and heed her voice, her insistent presence upon the earth, in the midst of those oppressed, driven from their homes, enslaved, and destroyed, we will respond with love — great love both for the earth itself and for all her children. We are each called to burn, to be pillars of fire, to be God's presence, warming and transforming the world together. Listen to two persons who understood what this word of God is now calling forth in us:

> Throughout my whole life, during every moment I have lived, the world has gradually been taking on light and fire for me, until it has come to envelop me in one mass of luminosity, glowing from within, ... the purple flush of matter imperceptibly fading

into the gold of the spirit, to be lost finally in the incandescence of a personal universe.... This is what I have learnt from my contact with the earth — the diaphany of the divine at the heart of a glowing universe, the divine radiating from the depths of matter a-flame.

(Pierre Teilhard de Chardin)

We who taste in prayer and study the fire of God's truth and love for us are inescapably called to rise up impassioned for the world's healing.

(Catherine of Siena)

Today we must draw nearer to the burning bush, renew our baptismal covenants, and feast together on the flesh and blood of the Son of Man, caring for all in such a way that "our light will shine before others who see our good works, and so give praise to our Father in heaven" (Mt 5:16).

Prayer: Mary, help us to draw nearer to our God, to live in truth, freed from sin, in service to others most in need, with the burning love of our God. May we honor your words and imitate your obedience and unbounded love for all of the human race. We ask this in the name of the Trinity. Amen.

6 Mother of the Poor; Mary of the Magnificat

Mary goes simply, barefooted, as a servant. She steps lightly over the threshold, from one millennium to the next, from a hill of praise to a hill of pain, from one country to another, dancing between earth and heaven. She is Mary who sings as she walks, as she obeys, as she hastens to all those in need of her voice, her submissiveness, her presence, her prayers, and the one she carries safely beneath her heart. She is a woman missioned, Spirit-driven, Spirit-led.

Magnificat! She stands in freedom! She has paradoxically stood at the cross as *stabat mater dolorosa*. She has stood in the shadow of the sword that pierced her soul to its roots, and she has stood in the shining mercy of the Holy One of God, her child risen from the grave. She has stood on the threshold of two covenants, in the Cenacle and the Upper Room, on the threshold of the church and the world. Now she stands on the threshold of the whole universe and the threshold of every human's heart, before every child of God.

She comes toward us, she comes in search of those who need her most: the poor, the enslaved, the ones running from violence, the destitute and the desperate, the hungry, the indigenous, all those who cross thresholds of race and religion, and especially the ones who die reaching out for life and tenderness. She comes to throw her mantle of justice over all, to embrace and draw us all closer to her heart and to the heartbeat of her firstborn child, Jesus the Christ. In the words of St. Ambrose, although "Christ has only one mother in the flesh, we all bring forth Christ in faith. Every soul receives the Word of God." We are each born to be both child and mother, as she was in her life.

Prayer: You, Mary, are the music of God. Your presence moves on all the roads, and you step first over the thresholds of the homes of the poor. In your dark countenance and strong hands God's flesh is exposed and we know we are loved, saved, and embraced by God in the light that dawns upon us in your great "Yes." In imitation of your stance before God, may we stand open-hearted with arms extended toward one another. May we who are born of grace be the beloved children of God and your children who walk to every corner of the earth. Amen.

7 A Prayer to Mary

Stillness of God, settle in our souls. Breath of God, move through us. Light of God, illumine our nights and dawn in our hearts. Shadow of God, fall over us as once you bent over the face of Mary and sow the seed of holiness, of justice, and of mercy within us. Whisper of love and truth in our waiting hearts. As we have gazed on these faces and forms of light, make us icons of your reflection for all the world to see. Mary, you who learned the wisdom of mercy and lived in its mystery, share that knowledge with us. May we hear again your words to all of us: "Do whatever he tells you!" (Jn 2:5). Give us the courage to walk through the world, intent on giving birth to your Word, your hope, and your love, steadfast until we find ourselves gathered into you, O Trinity, at home with this woman who believed, exalting together in the fullness of the freedom of the children of God. Amen.

Also available in the same series:

Three Minutes for the Soul
Reflections to Start the Day
Gerhard Bauer
ISBN: 978-1-56548-275-3, 72 pages

Mary
Four Weeks with the Mother of Jesus
Edited by Wolfang Bader and Stephen Liesenfeld
ISBN: 978-1-56548-281-6, 72 pages

Peace of Heart
Reflections on Choices in Daily Life
Marc Foley
ISBN: 978-1-56548-293-7, 72 pages

Pathways to God
Four Weeks on Faith, Hope and Charity
Robert F. Morneau
ISBN: 978-1-56548-286-9, 72 pages

Pathways to Community
Four Weeks on Prudence, Justice, Fortitude and Temperance
Robert F. Morneau
ISBN: 978-1-56548-303-3, 72 pages

Pathways to Relationship
Four Weeks on Simplicity, Gentleness, Humility, Friendship
Robert F. Morneau
ISBN: 978-1-56548-317-0, 72 pages

Sister Earth
Creation, Ecology and the Spirit
Helder Camara
ISBN: 978-1-56548-299-9, 72 pages

To order call 1-800-462-5980
or e-mail orders@newcitypress.com